WORLD OF WORK

HOSPITALITY & TOURISM

Exploring Career Pathways

Diane Lindsey Reeves

Created and produced by
Bright Futures Press, Cary, North Carolina
www.brightfuturespress.com

Published by
Cherry Lake Publishing, Ann Arbor, Michigan
www.cherrylakepublishing.com

Photo Credits: Cover, Beautyline; page 7, Africa Studios, Monkey Business Images, Rawpixel.com, Kzenon, Angelo Giampiccolo, Everything, Ekaphon maneechot, VG Stockstudio, page 8, Africa Studios; page 10, Monkey Business Images; page 12, Rawpixel.com; page 14, Kzenon; page 16, Alexey Y. Petrov; page 18, Everything; page 20, Ekaphon manneechot; page 22, VG Stockstudio; page 24, SointseRA.

Library of Congress Cataloging-in-Publication Date

CIP data has been filed and is available at catalog.loc.gov.

Printed in the United States of America.

TABLE OF CONTENTS

Hello, World of Work 4

Take a Hike 6

WoW Up Close 7

- Chef 8
- Concierge 10
- Event Planner 12
- Golf Pro 14
- Pilot 16
- Resort Manager 18
- Tourism Director 20
- Travel Agent 22

WoW Big List 24

Take Your Pick 26

Explore Some More 27

My WoW 30

Glossary 31

Index 32

HELLO WORLD OF WORK

This is you.

Right now, your job is to go to school and learn all you can.

This is the world of work.

It's where people earn a living, find purpose in their lives, and make the world a better place.

Sooner or later, you'll have to find your way from

HERE to THERE.

To get started, take all the jobs in the incredibly enormous world of work and organize them into an imaginary pile. It's a big pile, isn't it? It would be pretty tricky to find the perfect job for you among so many options.

No worries!

Some very smart career experts have made it easier to figure out. They sorted jobs and industries into groups by the types of skills and products they share. These groups are called career clusters. They provide pathways that will make it easier for you to find career options that match your interests.

- Architecture & Construction
- Arts & Communication
- Business & Administration
- Education & Training
- Finance
- Food & Natural Resources
- Government
- Health Sciences
- Hospitality & Tourism
- Human Services
- Information Technology
- Law & Public Safety
- Manufacturing
- Marketing, Sales & Service
- Science, Technology, Engineering & Mathematics (STEM)
- Transportation

Good thing you are still a kid.

You have lots of time to explore ideas and imagine yourself doing all kinds of amazing things. The **World of Work** (WoW for short) series of books will help you get started.

TAKE A HIKE!

There are 16 career pathways waiting for you to explore. The only question is: Which one should you explore first?

Is **Hospitality & Tourism** a good path for you to start exploring career ideas? There is a lot to like about this pathway. These professionals feed us and provide shelter when we are away from home. They provide rest, relaxation, and lots of fun when we are on vacation. They get us from place to place on trains, planes, ships, and automobiles.

See if any of the following questions grab your interest.

WOULD YOU ENJOY traveling, sightseeing, or meeting people from other countries?

CAN YOU IMAGINE someday working at a convention center, resort, or travel agency?

ARE YOU CURIOUS ABOUT what convention planners, golf pros, tour guides, resort managers, or wedding planners do?

If so, it's time to take a hike! Keep reading to see what kinds of opportunities you can discover along the Hospitality & Tourism pathway.

But wait!

What if you don't think you'll like this pathway?

You have two choices.

You could keep reading, to find out more than you already know. You might be surprised to learn how many amazing careers you'll find along this path.

OR

Turn to page 27 to get ideas about other WoW pathways.

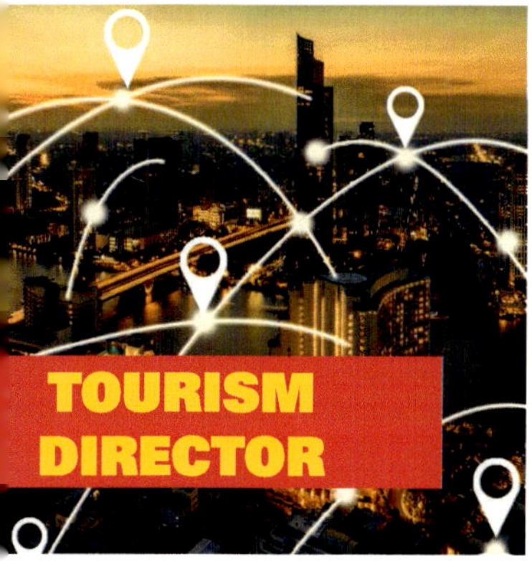

WoW Up Close

They whip up gourmet meals and serve them with a smile. They introduce us to the hot spots around town and help us plan fun vacations. They manage hotels, resorts, and convention centers. These are just some of the important jobs that people who work along the Hospitality & Tourism pathway do.

CHEF

Being a **chef** is like being an artist. Instead of using paints and easels, chefs create works of art with food. They work in the **culinary arts** and find new ways to amaze **foodies** with tasty dishes made from both ordinary and unusual ingredients. Chefs work in restaurants, hotels, and other places where fine food is favored.

There is a difference between being a cook and being a chef. It has to do with education and experience. Chefs typically have a culinary arts degree and have worked their way up through the ranks in a professional kitchen. They tend to make fancier food and often come up with their own creative recipes.

A chef's kitchen is a busy place with orders for all kinds of different meals coming in at the same time. Chefs work with other cooks and assistants to prepare each meal and present it in an appealing way. It is not unusual for a chef to repeat this process hundreds of times during a single **shift**. The pace is fast, and the work is demanding. The satisfaction comes when people rave about how much they enjoyed their meals.

This is one career can start preparing for before you grow up. You can learn how to cook right now in your family's kitchen. Get your parents' permission and give it a try! **Bon appetit!**

Check It Out!

Watch young chefs in action at

- http://www.fox.com/masterchef-junior
- http://www.foodnetwork.com/shows/chopped-junior

Start Now!

- Sign up for culinary arts classes in middle school and high school.
- Create a menu that includes a favorite food from each of your family members. Ask your parents for help preparing it.
- Save up your allowance and invite a friend to join you for a meal at a restaurant that serves a type of food you've never tried before. Thai, anyone?

CONCIERGE

So you've just arrived in a new town (or country!) and are checked in to a nice hotel. Your bags are unpacked, and you are ready to roll. How can you figure out out where all the hot spots to visit, tour, and eat are located?

Ask a **concierge**!

You can usually find a concierge working at a desk in the lobby of bigger, classy hotels or cruise ships. Some large corporations have concierges on staff to help employees make both business and personal travel and entertainment plans.

Concierges are experts at knowing what to do and where to go in their hometown. They make reservations for guests in fine restaurants and somehow manage to snag last-minute tickets to a play or concert. They help guests arrange transportation or find the most relaxing spa in town. In some cases, they may help guests with personal needs like finding a doctor or someone to repair a damaged garment.

Good customer service is the number one duty of concierges, so they must have good people skills. In some locations, it is helpful to speak more than one language. A college degree is not always required for this type of work. However, having a degree in hospitality management sometimes help people land the top jobs in fancier hotels.

Check It Out!

Visit the Web sites of some famous hotel chains and see which one you'd most want to stay (or work!) in.

- http://www.hilton.com
- http://www.marriott.com
- http://www.ritzcarlton.com
- http://www.omnihotels.com

Start Now!

- Put together a brochure that describes fun things to do and visit in your town.
- Make a list of tips for providing good customer service—for instance, using polite words like please and thank you.
- The next time your family visits a hotel, ask the concierge to tell you about local kid-friendly events.

EVENT PLANNER

Sometimes a cake, some candles, and a bunch of balloons are all you need to throw a party. Other times—say at a wedding or a major business convention—it takes quite a bit more planning. That's when it's time to call in an **event planner**.

Event planners are hired when events are so big or so important that they need a professional who knows what it takes to throw a big bash. The event might be a once-in-a-lifetime celebration, a community-wide festival, or a large conference. Whatever the occasion, event planners bring creative ideas, super-duper organizational skills, and knowledge on where to get the best supplies and service in town.

Event planners also organize the logistics of the event. If it's a wedding, they plan the order of events, from the time the bride walks down the aisle until the happy couple leaves for their honeymoon. If it's a big convention, they plan everything — registering guests, setting up the exhibit hall, putting up signs, and much more!

Some of the things event planners need to know can only be learned through experience and working alongside seasoned professionals. A college degree in hospitality or certification in event planning provides an edge for landing jobs in this field.

Check It Out!

Go online to find information about big events in your community or local convention center.

Start Now!

- Plan a birthday bash for a friend or family member complete with menus, activities, and a special theme.
- Make a to-do checklist that your family can use to stay organized when planning a holiday meal or party.
- Volunteer to help with decorations for your next school dance or holiday celebration.

GOLF PRO

There are pro golfers and **golf pros**. Pro golfers play golf for a living. They compete in **tournaments** in one or more of the world's professional tours (like the PGA, or Professional Golfers' Association of America). Golf pros teach golf for a living. In both cases, these players must play at the top of their game and know what it takes to win. Both types of pros must pass strict requirements and achieve PGA certification to be considered legit.

Golf pros run golf courses. They might work at a country club, a public driving range or golf course, or resort. Other golf pros coach teams at high schools or colleges. Those who work at golf courses often have many different responsibilities. A big part of their job is teaching people of all ages how to play. They might teach a class of young beginners in the morning and run a clinic on putting skills for advanced adults in the afternoon. Weekends are sometimes devoted to hosting golf tournaments.

In addition to teaching, golf pros are often involved in managing the golf course or the pro shop, which is where golf equipment is sold. Obviously, you don't need a college degree to play the game of golf. However, a college background is helpful and often required for a golf pro. Getting a degree in business or sports management prepares golf pros for the business side of the job.

By the way, tennis, skiing, and swimming are just a few examples of other sports where people turn to pros to improve their skills.

Check It Out!

Get the latest golf news and follow the pros online at

- http://www.golfchannel.com

Start Now!

- Sign up for golf lessons at a local club or recreation center.
- Ask your parents if you can plan a family putt-putt golf outing.
- Go online to learn all you can about golfing rules and make your own golf rulebook.

PILOT

Ever since Orville and Wilbur Wright invented the first airplane that could actually fly, people have been flying all over the world—and even to outer space! Flying makes it possible to have breakfast in New York City and dinner in Los Angeles on the same day.

Trips that once took weeks or months by ship or train can now be made in a matter of hours.

It's pretty amazing, and **pilots** make what seems impossible look easy. Think about it. Pilots step into the cockpit of a jet. They check the weather and conduct important safety inspections. They talk to the control tower and double-check their route. After the plane is filled with passengers and cargo—and a flight attendant gives a safety demonstration—they rev up the engine and roll down the runway. Then it's up, up, and way into the wide-open blue skies.

At this point, it is up to the pilot to get the plane, its passengers, and its contents safely to their intended destination. But pilots are prepared. They must pass intensive training before they can be licensed to fly. All commercial pilots must earn a college degree in aviation, aeronautical engineering, or a related field. Many commercial pilots get their start as military pilots, so they know their way around high-flying jets.

Check It Out!

Explore how airplanes work at

- http://bit.ly/PlanesFly1
- http://bit.ly/PlanesFly2
- http://bit.ly/PlanesFly3

Start Now!

- Visit an airport and watch the planes come and go.
- Find ideas for making your own paper airplanes at http://www.foldnfly.com.
- Learn all you can about different types of airplanes used by airlines and the military.

RESORT MANAGER

Resort managers do many of the same things that hotel managers do. They run the day-to-day operations of a place where guests come to sleep, eat, and enjoy special events. The big difference is that resort managers do their work in places where people really, really want to be. Think tropical paradise like Hawaii or the Bahamas. Think awesome amusement hangout like Disney World.

Resorts typically offer extras that even the nicest hotels don't have. Sure, they both may have soothing **spas** and outstanding places to dine. But resorts also have recreation in abundance. Pools with an ocean view. Golf and tennis and other recreational sports. Maybe the resort is located in the mountains with ski-in, ski-out access to winter fun. Maybe it's a dude ranch with horses and trails. The options are endless.

All this fun adds extra responsibilities for a resort manager to, um, manage. Which is why a college degree in hotel or hospitality management is so important. It is up to the resort manager to make sure that everything in the resort—from the minute guests arrive until they leave—runs smoothly and makes a good impression. This includes the front desk where guests are welcomed and registered, the clean and comfortable rooms where they stay, the restaurants where they eat, and all the places where they work and play.

Being a good manager means hiring and training good people to do their jobs well. A resort manager knows they have done a good job when guests enjoy their visit so much that they don't want to leave.

Check It Out!

Go online to explore the "world's best resorts."

Start Now!

- Dream up ideas for a resort that would appeal to kids your age. Make a brochure to advertise it.
- Make a list of all the places in the world you would one day like to visit.
- Ask your parents and grandparents to tell you about the best hotel or resort they ever visited.

TOURISM DIRECTOR

Imagine that you live in a really cool place. It's a big city with a bustling downtown. There are out-of-the-ordinary places to shop and eat and fun things to do. There is a sports stadium nearby, and a major sports team is on a winning streak. Excellent museum exhibits, plays, and concerts keep things interesting.

Not only is your city a great place to live, it's a great place to visit...

If only people knew to come.

Getting the word out about what a city has to offer is what **tourism directors** do. They often work for the city itself, the local **chamber of commerce**, or a convention center. Their job is to get people to visit—and spend money while they are there.

Marketing is a big part of the job. Tourism directors craft magazine ads, commercials, brochures, and social media activities to shine a spotlight on all their city has to offer. They make presentations to business groups looking for a great place to host a convention. They plan special events and attend conferences. The job involves lots of variety and takes lots of energy!

Since this is such a big job, it takes years of education and experience to get ready for it. A college degree in hospitality or business is a good first step.

Check It Out!

Find a conference center near you at

http://bit.ly/ConfCen

Start Now!

- Make a poster showing the top five reasons to visit your real (or imaginary!) city.
- Offer to take a friend on a tour of your neighborhood. Be sure to highlight all the points of interest.
- Check the newspapers for calendar listings of local festivals and fairs.

TRAVEL AGENT

Let's say you've just hit the jackpot and have enough money to take your entire family (and a couple of friends) on a dream vacation. It's a big surprise, and you want to get everything lined up before you tell anyone.

You'll need airline tickets, hotels, rental cars, and tickets for special entertainment. You go online to some popular travel Web sites and before you know it, you are...

Totally confused!

Travel Web sites are great for basic travel needs, but when it comes to planning a big trip for multiple people, it's time to call a **travel agent**. Travel agents make travel arrangements for people and businesses. They book transportation and lodging, arrange tickets to special activities, and plan **itineraries**. Travel agents often have the "inside scoop" on various destinations and can help clients find the best options for the best price.

When they are finished, all the client has to do is show up—and pay. Sometimes travel agents charge a fee for their services. But since hotels, cruise ships, and other **venues** often pay **commissions**, it usually doesn't cost much more to use a travel agent than it does to book all these services yourself.

It's like having a tour guide lead you to the perfect vacation!

Check It Out!

Do some online surfing and visit travel Web sites like

- http://www.expedia.com
- http://www.hotwire.com
- http://www.orbitz.com
- http://www.priceline.com
- http://www.travelocity.com

Start Now!

- Plane, train, ship, or automobile? Make a chart comparing the benefits of traveling by each mode of transportation.
- Make an itinerary for a trip you'd like to take to an extra-special place.

Activity director • Adventure travel guide • Airline ticket agent • Amusement and recreation attendant • Animal trainer • Baggage handler • Baggage porter • Baker • Banquet manager • Barista • Bartender • Bellhop • Bingo clerk • Bus driver • Carhop • Casino cage cashier • Casino dealer • Casino manager • Casino runner • Casino slot attendant • Caterer • Catering director • Catering manager • Certified personal chef • Chauffeur • **CHEF** • Collections manager • **CONCIERGE** • Conference planner • Conference service manager • Conservator • Convention service manager • Co-pilot • Corporate travel coordinator • Counter

WoW Big List

Take a look at some of the different kinds of jobs people do in the Hospitality & Tourism pathway. **WoW!**

Some of these job titles will be familiar to you. Others will be so unfamiliar that you will scratch your head and say "huh?"

attendant • Crew trainer • Cruise ship activities director • Cruise ship captain • Custodian • Customer service agent • Deli clerk • Desk clerk • Dining room supervisor • Dishwasher • Docent • Dry cleaner • Entertainer • Environmental services supervisor • **EVENT PLANNER** • Facilities manager • Food and beverage manager • Food service manager • Food service specialist • Food service worker • Front desk supervisor • Fry cook • Golf caddy • **GOLF PRO** • Greeter • Guest services representative • Guest services supervisor • Head cook • Head waiter • Historical interpreter • Hospitality coordinator • Host/hostess • Hotel maintenance manager • Hotel manager • Housekeeper • Innkeeper • Interpreter • Janitor • Kitchen steward • Laundry attendant • Lifeguard • Line cook • Line server • Meeting planner • National sales director • Navigator • Night auditor • Pastry chef • **PILOT** • Pizza maker • Prep cook • Private chef • Receptionist • Recreation leader • Referee • Reservation agent • Residence director • **RESORT MANAGER** • Restaurant general

Find a job title that makes you curious. Type the name of the job into your favorite Internet search engine and find out more about the people who have that job.

1. What do they do?
2. Where do they work?
3. How much training do they need to do this job?

manager • Restaurateur • Ride operator • Scuba diver instructor • Server • Ski instructor • Ski lift operator • Skycap • Sous chef • Station agent • Taxi driver • Telephone operator • Tennis pro • Ticket agent • Tour bus driver • Tour guide • **TOURISM DIRECTOR** • Tour sales representative • Train conductor• Train engineer • Translator • **TRAVEL AGENT** • Umpire • Usher • Valet • Waiter/Waitress

TAKE YOUR PICK

	Put stars next to your 3 favorite career ideas	Put an X next to the career idea you like the least	Put a question mark next to the career idea you want to learn more about
Chef			
Concierge			
Event planner			
Golf pro			
Pilot			
Resort manager			
Tourism director			
Travel agent			

What do you like most about these careers?	What is it about this career that doesn't appeal to you?	What do you want to learn about this career? Where can you find answers?

Which Big Wow List ideas are you curious about?

Please do **NOT** write in this book if it doesn't belong to you. You can download a copy of this activity online at www.brightfuturespress.com/teacher-guides.

EXPLORE SOME MORE

The Hospitality & Tourism pathway is only one of 16 career pathways that hold exciting options for your future. Take a look at the other 15 to figure out where to start exploring next.

Architecture & Construction

WOULD YOU ENJOY making things with LEGOs™, building a treehouse or birdhouse, or designing the world's best skate park?

CAN YOU IMAGINE someday working at a construction site, a design firm, or a building company?

ARE YOU CURIOUS ABOUT what civil engineers, demolition technicians, heavy-equipment operators, landscape architects, or urban planners do?

Arts & Communication

WOULD YOU ENJOY drawing your own cartoons, using your smartphone to make a movie, or writing articles for the student newspaper?

CAN YOU IMAGINE someday working at a Hollywood movie studio, a publishing company, or a television news station?

ARE YOU CURIOUS ABOUT what actors, bloggers, graphic designers, museum curators, or writers do?

Business & Administration

WOULD YOU ENJOY playing Monopoly, being the boss of your favorite club or team, or starting your own business?

CAN YOU IMAGINE someday working at a big corporate headquarters, government agency, or international business center?

ARE YOU CURIOUS ABOUT what brand managers, chief executive officers, e-commerce analysts, entrepreneurs, or purchasing agents do?

Education & Training

WOULD YOU ENJOY babysitting, teaching your grandparents how to use a computer, or running a summer camp for neighbor kids in your backyard?

CAN YOU IMAGINE someday working at a college counseling center, corporate training center, or school?

ARE YOU CURIOUS ABOUT what animal trainers, coaches, college professors, guidance counselors, or principals do?

Finance

WOULD YOU ENJOY earning and saving money, being the class treasurer, or playing the stock market game?

CAN YOU IMAGINE someday working at an accounting firm, bank, or Wall Street stock exchange?

ARE YOU CURIOUS ABOUT what accountants, bankers, fraud investigators, property managers, or stockbrokers do?

Food & Natural Resources

WOULD YOU ENJOY exploring nature, growing your own garden, or setting up a recycling center at your school?

CAN YOU IMAGINE someday working at a national park, raising crops in a city farm, or studying food in a laboratory?

ARE YOU CURIOUS ABOUT what landscape architects, chefs, food scientists, environmental engineers, or forest rangers do?

Government

WOULD YOU ENJOY reading about U.S. presidents, running for student council, or helping a favorite candidate win an election?

CAN YOU IMAGINE someday working at a chamber of commerce, government agency, or law firm?

ARE YOU CURIOUS about what mayors, customs agents, federal special agents, intelligence analysts, or politicians do?

Health Sciences

WOULD YOU ENJOY nursing a sick pet back to health, dissecting animals in a science lab, or helping the school coach run a sports clinic?

CAN YOU IMAGINE someday working at a dental office, hospital, or veterinary clinic?

ARE YOU CURIOUS ABOUT what art therapists, doctors, dentists, pharmacists, and veterinarians do?

Human Services

WOULD YOU ENJOY showing a new kid around your school, organizing a neighborhood food drive, or being a peer mediator?

CAN YOU IMAGINE someday working at an elder care center, fitness center, or mental health center?

ARE YOU CURIOUS ABOUT what elder care center directors, hairstylists, personal trainers, psychologists, or religious leaders do?

Information Technology

WOULD YOU ENJOY creating your own video game, setting up a Web site, or building your own computer?

CAN YOU IMAGINE someday working at an information technology start-up company, software design firm, or research and development laboratory?

ARE YOU CURIOUS ABOUT what artificial intelligence scientists, big data analysts, computer forensic investigators, software engineers, or video game designers do?

Law & Public Safety

WOULD YOU ENJOY working on the school safety patrol, participating in a mock court trial at school, or coming up with a fire escape plan for your home?

CAN YOU IMAGINE someday working at a cyber security company, fire station, police department, or prison?

ARE YOU CURIOUS ABOUT what animal control officers, coroners, detectives, firefighters, or park rangers do?

Manufacturing

WOULD YOU ENJOY figuring out how things are made, competing in a robot-building contest, or putting model airplanes together?

CAN YOU IMAGINE someday working at a high-tech manufacturing plant, engineering firm, or global logistics company?

ARE YOU CURIOUS ABOUT what chemical engineers, industrial designers, supply chain managers, robotics technologists, or welders do?

Marketing, Sales & Service

WOULD YOU ENJOY keeping up with the latest fashion trends, picking favorite TV commercials during Super Bowl games, or making posters for a favorite school club?

CAN YOU IMAGINE someday working at an advertising agency, corporate marketing department, or retail store?

ARE YOU CURIOUS ABOUT what creative directors, market researchers, media buyers, retail store managers, and social media consultants do?

Science, Technology, Engineering & Mathematics (STEM)

WOULD YOU ENJOY concocting experiments in a science lab, trying out the latest smartphone, or taking advanced math classes?

CAN YOU IMAGINE someday working in a science laboratory, engineering firm, or research and development center?

ARE YOU CURIOUS ABOUT what aeronautical engineers, ecologists, statisticians, oceanographers, or zoologists do?

Transportation

WOULD YOU ENJOY taking pilot or sailing lessons, watching a NASA rocket launch, or helping out in the school carpool lane?

CAN YOU IMAGINE someday working at an airport, mass transit system, or shipping port?

ARE YOU CURIOUS ABOUT what air traffic controllers, flight attendants, logistics planners, surveyors, and traffic engineers do?

MY WoW

I am here.

Name

Grade

School

Who I am.

Make a word collage! Use 5 adjectives to form a picture that describes who you are.

Where I'm going.

The next career pathway I want to explore is

Some things I need to learn first to succeed.

1

2

3

To get here.

Please do **NOT** write in this book if it doesn't belong to you. You can download a copy of this activity online at www.brightfuturespress.com/teacher-guides.

GLOSSARY

bon appetit
a French phrase that means "enjoy your meal"

chamber of commerce
an association of businesspeople that promotes business in the local community

chef
person who is a professional cook

commissions
fees paid to agents for performing a service

concierge
person who helps hotel guests by providing information and assistance

convention
a formal gathering of people who have the same profession or interest

culinary arts
the art of preparing, cooking, and presenting food

event planner
person who organizes social and business events

foodies
people with an enthusiastic interest in food, especially gourmet foods

golf pro
person who teaches others how to play golf and/or runs a golf course

itineraries
plans for a trip

logistics
the handling of the details of an operation

pilot
person who is qualified to operate an airplane

resort manager
person who oversees the day-to-day operations of a really nice place where people go for rest and recreation

shift
a period of several hours of continuous work

spas
facilities devoted to health, fitness, weight loss, beauty, and relaxation

tourism director
person in charge of attracting visitors to a certain city or region

tournaments
series of contests between a number of competitors, who compete for an overall prize

travel agent
person who helps people and businesses plan trips and make travel arrangements

venues
places where events are held

INDEX

Architecture & Construction, 5, 27
Arts & Communication, 5, 27
Bahamas, 18
*Boeing, 17
Business Administration, 5, 27
*Chopped Junior, 9
Disney World, 18
Education & Training, 5, 27
*Expedia, 23
Finance, 5, 28
*Fold'NFly, 17
Food & Natural Resources, 5, 28
*Golf Channel, 15
Government, 5, 28,
Hawaii, 18
Health Science, 5, 28
*Hilton, 11
Hospitality & Tourism, 5
*Hotwire, 23
*HowStuffWorks, 17
Human Resources, 5, 28
Information Technology, 5, 28
Law & Public Safety, 5, 29
*Learn Engineering, 17
Manufacturing, 5, 29
*Marriott, 11
*MasterChef Junior, 9
*Omni Hotels and Resorts, 11
*Orbitz, 23
*Priceline, 23
*Ritz-Carlton, 11
Science, Technology, Engineering & Mathematics, 5, 29
*Smart Meetings, 21
*TestTube Plus, 17
Transportation, 5, 29
*Travelocity, 23

*** Refers to the Web page sources**

About the Author

Diane Lindsey Reeves is the author of lots of children's books. She has written several original PEANUTS stories (published by Regnery Kids and Sourcebooks). She is especially curious about what people do and likes to write books that get kids thinking about all the cool things they can be when they grow up. She lives in Cary, North Carolina, and her favorite thing to do is play with her grandkids—Conrad, Evan, Reid, and Hollis Grace.